KV-087-886

Singing in special schools

by David Ward
organiser of the Music for Slow Learners Project

The Music for Slow Learners Project is sponsored
by the Carnegie United Kingdom Trust and based at
Dartington College of Arts

Published for the Standing Conference for
Amateur Music
by the **Bedford Square Press**
of the National Council of Social Service
26 Bedford Square London WCIB 3HU

© SCAM 1973

ISBN 0 7199 0880 9

HERTFORDSHIRE
COUNTY LIBRARY

6357072
371.926

JUL 1979
HERTFORDSHIRE
COUNTY MUSIC LIBRARY
WELWYN GARDEN CITY

Distributed by RPS Limited
Victoria Hall East Greenwich London SE10 0RF
Design and typography by NCSS Publications Department
Printed in England by Bowering Press Limited Plymouth

Members of the Project's Steering Committee

R L Bishop, *Chairman*	*Lately, Warden of Beaumont Hall, University of Leicester*
Sir Bernard de Bunsen	*Chairman of the Consultative Committee of the Church of England Colleges of Education*
P Cox	*Principal, Dartington College of Arts*
W Drabble	*HMI*
L W Downes	*Head of Education Department, St Luke's College, Exeter*
M E V Lane	*Tutor in charge of Music Education, Dartington College of Arts*
P C Love	*Senior Adviser and County Educational Psychologist, Devon County Education Committee*
J K Owens	*Director, National Council of Social Service*
J P B Dobbs	*Director of the Project, Director of Musical Studies, Dartington College of Arts*
J D Ward	*Organiser of the Project*
Miss D Osborne	*Secretary to the Steering Committee*

Singing in special schools

This book is about singing. It is intended to give guidance to teachers who work with children receiving special education. The term 'slow learners' is used to describe children with various degrees of mental handicap found in ESN schools, in schools for the physically handicapped and in special classes attached to primary and secondary schools. Most of the suggestions offered are equally applicable to normal children, and experienced teachers will recognize some of the well tried techniques described—techniques which make for enjoyable and efficient singing sessions. With slow learning children it is essential for singing to be enjoyable and for the teaching to be effective.

Where possible the suggestions are related to specific groups—e.g. children in ESN schools, SSN children in these schools, but occasionally it is necessary to refer more generally to slow learning or handicapped children. It is hoped that the reader will recognise the difficulty of making generalisations, and realise the very wide range and varying degree of ability in any group of children in a special educational setting.

I would like to acknowledge the contributions and help given to me by the teachers and lecturers who have worked on the Music for Slow Learners project, in particular Jon Cooke, Avis Butler, Ann Hunt, Margaret Johnson, Michael Lane, Jane Mayers and Reina Seifert. I am grateful to Jack Dobbs and to Charles Cleall for helping me to compile this booklet and especially grateful for the enthusiasm and support of all the children who are involved in making music with us.

It could be said that any children who are denied the opportunity to sing are deprived of the most important means of musical expression. In particular, children who are slow learners by reason of mental or physical handicap can derive great enjoyment from singing; through this enjoyment they gain an enriching experience and our relationship with them is strengthened.

There are many reasons why slow learners should be encouraged to sing. Singing can help them to attain a good posture, it can assist breathing and help to keep bronchial and nasal passages clear. Language and speech are clearly improved by singing and some teachers have found that children can make positive gains in reading attainment through songs. Many music educators believe that singing is the best way of training the ear; a keen and alert aural sense will help the children to develop an increased appreciation of music and a more sensitive attitude to the world about them, particularly where sound is concerned. Charles Cleall* believes that 'the cultivation of the voice . . . is not only delightful but the best means of training the ear, even of the tone dumb'. The benefits of singing are well described by Jack Dobbs in *The slow learner and music* (OUP). In particular, he suggests that much can be learnt about the world in general from the words of songs.

Some teachers of severely subnormal children have found that certain of their most difficult children can be reached by singing questions and instructions to them. For some reason, these children respond to this technique rather than to the more usual methods.

In the past it was sometimes considered that slow learners were so poor at singing that it was hardly worth while to teach them to sing at all. There are a number of reasons for this, including the following:
i) The mis-use of the piano. Generally speaking, children do not find it easy to learn songs from melodic patterning on the piano. The sustaining power of the average piano is poor and in any case the piano cannot teach the shaping of words and phrases of songs. Some head-teachers have wrongly believed that their teachers cannot teach singing if they have no keyboard skill.
ii) The teacher's lack of confidence in using her own voice. This may be why the piano is mis-used. The most efficient way to teach songs is by singing them to the children.
iii) Too much reliance upon school song books. Songs in school books can become dated and many are arranged in keys which are too high for the majority of slow learning children who need considerable experience in using the lower range of their voices before they are ready to sing higher notes with confidence.
iv) Too great a concern with the production of a 'good' tone. Slow learners tend to have rather 'rough' voices which can sound quite exciting if developed in the lower vocal range. Also, the type of songs which are related to their own experience are more appropriately sung using a tone which is not over 'cultivated'.

Recent experience in schools shows that severely subnormal, educationally subnormal and 'remedial' class children can sing complete, lengthy songs and that their performance compares very favourably with that of normal children. One ESN school has successfully performed a 'pop' cantata involving 1,500 words. Another special school has a

* *Voice production in choral technique*   Novello

repertoire of over 100 songs, some of which are in three parts. A small choir of SSN children recently sang six carols involving thirty-five verses. ESN school choirs are included in a number of English school music festivals in which they take part quite adequately, learning and singing their parts along with normal children.

How can good singing develop in a school? The following suggestions are based on recent experience in a number of special schools in which singing is a well established activity.

THE NEED FOR CONTINUITY

When children join their school at the age of five or six they do not normally reject singing for emotional reasons. On the whole they are ready to sing, and at this stage the problem is that of finding enough simple material. A good start can be made with nursery rhymes. Remember that many children who come from poorer homes may not have had the valuable experience of mother singing to them as infants. The reception class teacher may need to refresh her own memory of nursery rhymes, revising and practising them unaccompanied if possible. *The Oxford nursery song book* (OUP) will help here, but the teacher should not allow the book to fix the key; song books usually pitch songs too high for beginners. A number of investigations, including one with ESN children,* have been made suggesting that a comfortable range for young children with inexperienced voices is from A1 to A—i.e. one octave around middle C. Thus, *Baa baa black sheep* or *Twinkle twinkle little star* or *My three hens*—all very similar—might begin on A1 or Bb1 just below middle C.

For additional nursery songs it is well worth consulting *American folk songs for children* (Doubleday). *Johnny get your hair cut* and *Mary wore her red dress* are examples of songs from this book which young children enjoy. Most of these American songs have actions and simple movements which add interest and possibly more meaning to the songs. At this stage it would be useful to give the children some of the street and playground games and rhymes which they might otherwise miss by being educated separately from normal children who quite naturally pass on their own folk lore. Teachers who are interested in creating simple melodies with their children might consider using the words of these rhymes, e.g. 'It's raining, it's pouring, the old man's snoring'. There are collections of street and playground rhymes for reference—see Peter and Iona Opie's *Lore and language of school children* and *Children's*

---

* Cleall, C, *Voice production in choral technique*   Novello
  Ward, D, *Sound approaches for slow tearners*   Bedford Square Press

games in street and playground (OUP). Also, Topic Records have produced many of these rhymes on a disc entitled *Children's singing games* (Mary Wilson and Jennifer Gallagher, Impact IMP—A 101). The teacher will remember some of these including *The farmer's in his den, Poor Mary lies a-weeping* and *Make the bed, turn the pillows over*, and some teachers from the north of England might remember 'dandling' songs sung to them by their parents or grandparents.

Having made a start with the youngest children, the school might plan to provide opportunities for the children to sing their known songs and to add new ones gradually as they move through the junior stage and into the secondary stage. In order to do this they need regular opportunities, perhaps not the traditional two 30 minute weekly lessons but certainly several weekly occasions when songs can be enjoyed. In schools where a particular teacher has a strong interest in music short periods of class exchanges might be planned. Additionally, other teachers might be encouraged to initiate singing sessions preferably at a suitable time of day when the children are ready for a change of activity or need to be prepared for an occasion. Most head teachers would be horrified if reading or number skills were taught in an isolated and unsystematic way. Continuity of content and approach is just as important in music as it is in any other activity.

New songs will be needed as the children develop through the junior stage. There are plenty of school song books available, but these need not be the only source of material. There is at present a good supply of folk songs on records. In particular, folk groups like The Spinners, which attract a wide audience, have recorded songs which are catchy and singable. Certain songs which appear in the Top Twenty emerge from time to time having a particularly strong quality, and they may make a deeper impact upon the children than is sometimes believed. Useful collections of songs are listed in the appendix to this book. Especially useful books are *Sing together* and *The Oxford school music books, junior series*, both published by OUP.

Few ESN schools have all their very oldest children singing regularly, apart from the hymn singing at morning worship. In many SSN schools one hears the oldest children singing, but unfortunately some of these older children are not encouraged to progress to songs suited to their emotional level. It is not a good idea to persist with singing sessions with children who are not keen; it is better to organise singing on an optional basis, perhaps in a lunch hour or as a club activity. The school choir might be one of these school club activities. A number of ESN schools have established a choir consisting of children from the middle and upper age ranges. These choirs mostly begin with about twenty children selected on the basis of vocal ability and enthusiasm. They meet at lunch times and at times when it is convenient to withdraw from classes. Having started with a small number of children, these choirs tend to grow in size as other children notice the enjoyment and sense of achievement of their friends together with the fact that they sometimes go out to festivals and concerts. The repertoire of the choir can be more extensive and adventurous than that of the classroom and it is quite possible to have two-part singing in the choir. The following songs have been performed excellently by ESN school choirs:

Kumbayah—with an easy descant; *Michael, row the boat ashore; Green grow the rushes-o; Oh, sinner man; Lord of the dance; Thank you*—from *Faith, Folk and Clarity* (published by Galliard); *When I first came to this land; This little light of mine; I'm getting married in the morning*— from *My Fair Lady; Edleweiss* and *Doe, a deer*—from *The Sound of Music*; All the songs from *Joseph and the Amazing Technicolor Dreamcoat; I don't know how to love Him*—from *Jesus Christ Superstar.*
Rounds:
Why doesn't my goose sing as well as thy goose?; Row, row, row your boat; Kookaburra.

The sources of most of these songs are given in the appendix to this book.

TEACHING SONGS

It has been suggested already that the piano is not the best instrument to use to teach songs to children. One reason for this is that the melody might sound to the children like a succession of percussive sounds which do not flow easily into each other. Also, the piano gives little idea of the words and phrases of a song. This is not to decry the overall useful-ness of the piano in song teaching. Many teachers who have difficulty in singing at sight find it helpful to play the melody of songs to teach themselves in readiness for teaching the children. The sensitive addition of a simple accompaniment can give a song harmonic and rhythmic sense. Teachers who have a moderate keyboard skill might experiment with simple 'vamping' techniques in two or three keys. Some songbooks give guitar chords under the melody line and it is not difficult to devise a simple vamping piano accompaniment based upon the given chords. Robert Noble's books—*Three chords and beyond* and *European folk tunes* (Novello)—are very useful for the teacher's own use. The piano should not dictate the key of a song. A comfortable key which suits the range of the children's voices should be chosen, then an appropriate accompaniment may be devised. D major would be a very useful key to become familiar with; a number of the songs suggested above lie easily in this key—e.g. *Kumbayah*, *Michael row the boat ashore* and *When I first came to this land*.

The teacher's own voice is probably the best model for patterning a song. An unsteady voice can be helped to stay secure by quietly sounding a guitar string, chime bar or one piano note of appropriate pitch at phrase endings. With the younger children it is better to teach the songs without song books or word sheets; these will only distract and confuse. As they become more accustomed to responding to the printed word later on it is helpful to display the words printed on a large sheet of paper or card. This is preferable to individual word sheets at this stage because it will have the effect of keeping the children's heads up. It may be necessary to employ some help in pointing to the words to help them follow easily. Songs should be taught quickly, phrase by phrase, the children singing each phrase immediately back to the teacher without halting the pulse. Some teachers often begin by teaching the last phrase of a song. The children are then ready to join in with the part they know and each time it is sung they learn a little more of it. Songs which have choruses—e.g. *Lord of the dance*, lend themselves well to this kind of approach. The children might be invited to complete a phrase themselves. The teacher might sing, 'Here we go round the mulberry bush on a cold and . . .' stopping to allow the children to continue, 'frosty morning.' Most children enjoy doing this, indeed it is difficult to prevent them, when presented with a logical phrase. This technique has been used effectively with children who stutter and stammer. The rhythm and flow of the musical phrase seem to displace the emotional tension which often adds to the physical difficulties of children who stutter.

Many teachers, particularly those who work with SSN children, are rightly concerned about the tendency in their children to 'shout' their songs. This may be the result of enthusiasm, or lack of vocal flexibility or immature perception. This shouting tendency is difficult to overcome but it is helpful to teach the songs in low keys, to use a quiet vocal model and to provide a soft, mellow accompaniment. The guitar is an excellent instrument for this purpose. One or two open strings can provide a perfectly adequate accompaniment—e.g. open strings D and A can be used to accompany *This old man*.

This old man		He played one	
(D)	(D)	(D)	(D)

He	*played*	*knick*	*knack*	*on*	*my*	*drum*	
(A)		(A)		(A)		(A)	etc.

It is perfectly valid for the teacher to demonstrate displeasure at shouted songs; the difficulty lies in maintaining a good balance of enthusiasm and self-control.

Another problem which concerns teachers of slow learning children is monotone singing. The children who monotone need extra opportunities to use their voices and should not be withdrawn from singing classes. Some of them will, given time, naturally begin to modulate their voices, particularly if they are placed alongside their classmates who sing well. If the music activities are varied enough there will be occasions when they can feel the rise and fall of melodic phrases by simple movements and actions perhaps patterned by the teacher. Also, attentive listening to and involvement in making good sounds with everyday objects and instruments will help their perception to develop, thus making varied vocal sounds more possible. For suggestions about the use of sound see *Sound approaches for slow learners*, by David Ward (Bedford Square Press).

It is helpful to give individual 'growlers' a few minutes each day trying to match teacher's voice with theirs. 'Good morning' might be sung by the child followed by the teacher who will try to imitate the child's pitch and inflexions. Next, repeat the phrase by starting at the child's pitch but changing the note slightly up *and down*. Experiment with sliding, squealing and growling effects, inviting the child to try to imitate. In this way he will physically be able to feel his voice moving up and down, really *using* his voice. It has been observed that there are more monotone singers in those schools where singing happens infrequently—an obvious statement perhaps, but it illustrates the need for experience as a requirement for learning to take place.

The possibilities of using records to teach songs should not be overlooked. Many of our folk and popular singers (and comedians) have pleasing voices and should not be compared with trained 'classical' singers. Popular songs can sound quite incongruous when performed by trained singers and whilst one discourages imitations of popular clichés, some of the sounds produced by these performers can be used as models for children. Records which have been used effectively in this way include *Growing up with Wally Whyton* (Pye GGL 0285), *Gospel songs and spirituals for little children* (from the Salvation Army, 101 Queen Victoria Street, London EC4), *Songs for singing children* by John Langstaffe (EMI XLP 50008) and certain popular hits which have a limited life span—e.g. *Morning has broken*, recorded by Cat Stevens in 1972. Teachers of young children are recommended to try *Bang on a drum*, a BBC Playschool record (BBC—Roundabout No 17).

Often, singing sessions are best when they happen at the 'right' moment and when they finish at the 'right' moment—before the children lose interest or become fatigued. Many schools operate flexible time-tables allowing for spontaneity and suitable timing of activities. Opportunities should be taken to sing songs for an occasion such as a birthday or a seasonal event. For further suggestions on music for special occasions see chapter 7 of *The slow learner and music* by J P B Dobbs (OUP).

It is recognised that teachers may have to take music lessons for set periods owing to time-table requirements. Two 30 minute lessons per week is a common pattern. Singing might well occupy the whole half-hour period but it may be wiser to plan a number of short and varied music activities within the period, with singing as one of these activities. These will be more meaningful if they are related to a particular theme, say 'animals', about which songs can be sung, sounds made and listened to, rhythms based on animal names played, stories about animals with sound effects and simple accompaniments to animal songs invented and performed. A sample lesson of this kind is described in the appendix.

The school choir might devote the whole of a given period to singing. The session will be successful if the overall pace is kept brisk, with no pauses for talk. For much of the time known songs will be sung and enjoyed; new songs or sections of songs are best taught quickly and efficiently in the early part of the session, the repertoire being slowly extended over the term or year. Choir practice needs to move at a good pace with the minimum of talk from the teacher (and the children). Awkward pauses between songs should not happen—nothing is more frustrating than having to wait for the pianist/teacher to find the correct book and page. These, if needed, should be open and ready beforehand and word sheets should be displayed before the session starts. It is worthwhile studying the stage presentation of some of our professional entertainers to gain an understanding of pace and timing, two factors vitally important to the success of a choir practice. Songs which prove unexpectedly difficult might be abandoned in mid-stream, the teacher thus gaining time to reconsider the suitability of the song or teaching method. Often, ESN choirs learn a phrase wrongly the first time they hear it, and consequently relearning is very difficult. The teacher will have to decide whether to accept the fault and allow it to continue or to abandon the song and return to it later on. This is not to condone an incorrect or sloppy performance but there are some songs which become naturally varied over the years. The teacher's own standards and commitment to the children and the music will be the bases for such a decision.

It has already been suggested that a particular vocal tone may or may not be appropriate to any given song. Sea shanties are likely to sound odd if performed with a cathedral choirboy tone; on the other hand the children might be encouraged to produce a quiet pleasing tone when they attempt a slow lyrical melody. Most slow learning children have a particular richness in the lower vocal range or chest voice as it has been called (from about G next below middle C to E on the first line of the treble clef). Exciting sounds can be produced by the older children in ESN school choirs in this lower register. Individual boys and girls whose voices are changing can produce delightful sounds, and they may be encouraged to take solo verses and to play leading parts in school pantomimes and musicals. Luckily, perhaps, some of our ESN children do not have so many inhibitions about performing as brighter children. We should discourage unfair exploitation in pushing them to perform to an audience, but they can sometimes contribute greatly through their performances towards establishing a favourable attitude to them by the general public.

Many teachers consider part singing to be a worthy but impossible aim for their ESN choirs. A few children in the choir may have a 'natural' ear for harmony and a group of children might be formed to include these children who may be quite able to learn and sing a second part or descant. It is likely that the singing of rounds will give the children a taste for harmony but this cannot be taken for granted. Sometimes children sing rounds in a competitive way and have little musical under-standing of the whole. Unfortunately there are very few written part songs which are simple enough for our children. The imaginative teacher might try writing very simple second parts to well known songs for the children to learn. Sometimes descants or second parts are best learnt as independent melodies to be added to the main melody when the children are sufficiently confident in singing them. The teacher might experiment with the positioning of groups within the choir—it is not necessarily best to have them all facing the front. One choir was observed rehearsing their parts, each part standing in a circular formation. In this way the children felt their part was more unified. Quiet singing is necessary in order that they can become more aware of the other parts and of the whole harmonic effect. When children experience this for the first time, it is one of the finest delights in all music making.

Rounds can be taught using the circle formation and various ways of singing them might be tried. One way is to have each group constantly repeating one phrase of the round. This quickly becomes tedious, but it may help them to appreciate the harmony more easily. Another idea is to tape-record the whole group singing the round several times through (without stopping), replay and have the whole group sing against themselves. The teacher might experiment with the various points at which the second part may enter in the round. It is sometimes helpful to delay the second entry until the half-way point—e.g. in *Frere Jacques* the second entry starts when the first part reaches '*Sonnez (les matines)*'. It is difficult to know at what stage the children begin to appreciate the harmonic aspect of music making. It seems that there are wide individual differences in this but the perceptive teacher will know the stage at which her choir is ready to begin part singing. There is probably a stage of group readiness for this just as there is for other activities. Certainly it is better to have secure and confident unison singing than poor part singing.

The foregoing suggestions are based upon observations of and practical experience with children in a number of different schools. It is hoped that the reader of this booklet will not believe that they are infallible. From time to time certain teachers are observed using techniques and approaches which seem unsound but which produce unusually good results. These are often people who, by virtue of their personality and experience with handicapped children seem to be able to teach by almost any method. Valuable as it is to modify one's approach after seeing others at work, it is right for the teacher to develop her own personal approach. In special education in particular the first need is to make a good relationship with the children; they will respond to the *person*. Music can be an important factor in establishing this relationship. If it does nothing else but this it will have served a valuable purpose.

Appendix 1

The following notes relate to a session taken with a class of ESN school boys and girls aged 8–10 years.

Setting The children's own classroom. The children were seated in chairs in a horse-shoe arrangement.

Equipment 1 adequate piano, 1 guitar, 3 chime bars D, A, D^1, 2 triangles, 1 cymbal, 2 tambours, 4 small tom-tom drums, 2 wood-blocks, 3 maracas, 3 sheets of cartridge paper bearing the words of the song.

Preparation Instruments were put out on the floor in front of each chair. They were grouped according to sound quality—wood, metal, drums, shakers. The song sheet was attached to the blackboard for display.

The activities

1 Introductory song *One more river** in D major. The teacher sang the chorus of the song twice, then the whole song with the children joining in the chorus each time.

2 Some talk about animals. The children were asked to recall the animals in the song and to give as many names of other animals as they could.

3 Use of instruments. Each group—wood, metal, drums, shakers—was invited to make sounds for about ten seconds. The teacher suggested that the four tone qualities reminded him of different animal movements. The metallic sounds were like birds gliding, the wooden sounds like hens pecking, the drums like elephants and the maracas like snakes moving over small stones. The sounds were made again and four children moved to each group sound pretending to be the various animals.

4 The song *One more river* was repeated, the children making appropriate sounds during verse 1 (elephant), verse 2 (rhino), verse 3 (bear, flea and humble bee) and verse 6 (hyena and monkey).

5 Three children were given chime bars D, A and D^1 and were shown how and when to play in order to make a simple accompaniment for the song:

> One more river, and that's the river of Jordan
> (D)   (D)   (A)   (D)
>
> One more river, there's one more river to cross
> (D)   (D)   (A)   (D)

6 The whole song was repeated with sound effects for verses 1, 2, 3 and 6 and chime bar accompaniment for verses 4, 5, 7, 8, 9, 10. The guitar also accompanied the song using chords D major and A^7. The children sang each chorus.

* See appendix 2.

Appendix 2

The following listed songs have all been successfully performed by ESN or SSN children. The songs often appear in more than one song book; care has been taken to suggest the minimum number of books and to select versions which are well presented. It may be necessary to transpose many of the songs into keys which suit the children's vocal range.

SONGS FOR YOUNG CHILDREN

The Oxford nursery song book P Buck OUP
This book contains all the well-known nursery rhymes

American folk songs for children Ruth Seeger Doubleday

Mr Frog's wedding	The mocking bird song
Jimmy crack corn	Who built the ark?
Mary wore her red dress	Johnnie get your hair cut
Who's that tapping at the window?	There was a man and he was mad
The train is a'coming	

Music time Mabel Wilson OUP

Jackie the sailor	The donkey and the cuckoo
Susie, little Susie	

The Oxford school music books R Fiske and J Dobbs OUP
JUNIOR BOOK I

There's a young lad	Bobby Shaftoe
Sing said the mother	Boney was a warrior
The drummer and the cook	Down in Demerara
Go and tell Aunt Nancy	

JUNIOR BOOK 2

The keeper	Nelly Bly
O, soldier, soldier	Sourwood Mountain
Oh, my little Augustin	

JUNIOR BOOK 3
Donkey riding

Sixty songs for little children H Wiseman and J Wishart OUP
My three hens

Sing together W Appleby and F Fowler OUP

The gay musician	Jim along Josie
Ten in the bed	The barnyard song
This old man	Skip to my Lou
The noble Duke of York	The cuckoo
Tree in the wood	Michael Finnegan
Turn the glasses over	Leave her Johnny

Folk songs for fun   O Brand   Essex Music
The hole in the bucket   Aiken drum
Old MacDonald

Sing a merry song   B Swift and W Clauson   OUP
Let's all sing together

Nursery rhymes with a new look   Hazel Hudson   Edward Ashdown
Ernie the elephant

Sing a new song   Orff-Schulwerk   Schott
Looby loo   Row, row row your boat (round)

Children's play songs   P Nordoff   and   C Robbins   Theodore Presser   Company
Pennsylvania
all the songs from this book are suitable

SONGS FOR OLDER CHILDREN

Sing together   W Appleby and F. Fowler   OUP
Li'L Liza Jane   What shall we do with a drunken
A–roving   sailor?
John Brown's body   Fire down below
The mermaid   Waltzing Matilda
I'se the b'y that builds the boat   Green grow the rushes–o

Something to sing   G Brace   CUP
BOOK I
Jesse James   Casey Jones
Jamaica farewell   The sloop John B
This old hammer

BOOK 2
Yellow rose of Texas

A pentatonic song book   B Brocklehurst   Schott
Old Dan Tucker   Little David
Swing low sweet chariot   Land of the silver birch
One more river   The Derby ram

Faith, Folk and Clarity   ed by P Smith   Galliard
The Lord's prayer   Kumbayah
Lord of the dance   Go, tell it on the mountain
Thank you   Amen

124 Folk songs   Robbins Music Corporation

Down in the valley	Joshua fought the battle of Jericho
Oleanna	Red river valley
Tom Dooley	This little light of mine
Study war no more	Pick a bale o' cotton

104 Folk songs   Robbins Music Corporation

Oh, sinner man	Michael, row the boat ashore
We shall overcome	Streets of Laredo

Folk songs for fun   collected by O Brand   Essex Music

When the saints go marching in	Goodnight ladies
When I first came to this land	Ten green bottles
Alouette	Blow the man down
Pat works on the railway	

Songs of the new world   D MacMahon   McDougall

Home on the range	Johnny has gone for a soldier

Twelve folk songs from Jamaica   ed by T Murray   OUP

Wata come to me eye	Banana loader's song
Linstead market	

The American folksong book   Penguin Books

The hammer song	It takes a worried man to sing a worried song

The Oxford school music books   R Fiske and J Dobbs   OUP
JUNIOR BOOK 3
The lone star trail

The Oxford nursery song book   compiled by P Buck   OUP
Polly wolly doodle

American folk songs for children   Ruth Seeger   Doubleday
Mary had a baby

The singing island   P Seeger and E McColl   Schott
Johnny Todd

CANTATAS
Jonah man jazz   M Hurd   Novello
Joseph and the amazing technicolor dreamcoat   Rice and Webber   Novello

18

MUSICAL PLAYS
The midnight thief R Rodney Bennet Mills Music
The snow wolf M. Williamson Josef Weinberger

The following music books are recommended for further sources of songs, ideas for accompaniments and hints on teaching.

Sociable songs Books I and II ed by Anne Mendoza OUP
Songs with simple piano accompaniments; guitar chords and symbols; hints on teaching.

People who help us E Hughes Novello
Songs about the bus driver, policeman etc; easy piano accompaniments.

Things that help us E Hughes Novello
Songs about toys, books, cars etc.

Our friends the animals E Hughes Novello
Animal songs; easy piano accompaniments.

Music makers Stages 1, 2 and 3 Marion Berry Longmans
Mainly about the use of musical notation; large, clear print.

Rhymes with chimes Olive Rees and Anne Mendoza OUP
Simple songs with easy parts for chime bars and other percussion.

Children make music R Addison Holmes McDougall
A handbook of practical suggestions for a wide variety of music activities.

Ring a ding—Songs with tuned percussion Yvonne Adair Novello
Very simple two note accompaniments using chime bars.

Singing games for recreation Books I–IV Janet E Tobitt A & C Black
Well-known and unusual singing games, melody only with instructions for actions.

On the beat and beat two Anne Mendoza and Joan Rimmer Boosey & Hawkes
Simple melodies with 2 note accompaniments.

The Oxford school music books *Infant book* J Dobbs and W Firth.
The Oxford school music books *Teacher's manual* R Fiske and J Dobbs.
A variety of suggestions to help the music teacher including basic piano and recorder tuition.

An introduction to group music making G Winters Chappell
A handbook of advice and suggestions about the use of school instruments.

Children's traditional singing games Books 1–5 Gomme and Sharp Novello

The Clarendon book of singing games Books 1 & 2 H Wiseman and S Northcote
OUP

Children's games in street and playground P and I Opie OUP

Three chords and beyond   R Noble   Novello
A useful book for the teacher's own use; melodies with two and three chord accompaniments for guitar or piano.

The following books on music for handicapped children refer to singing :
The slow learner and music   J Dobbs   OUP
They can make music   P Bailey   OUP
Music for the handicapped child   Juliette Alvin   OUP
Therapy in music for handicapped children   P Nordoff and C Robbins   Gollancz
Music in schools   J B Brocklehurst   Routledge and Kegan Paul
Music therapy   J Alvin   John Baker Books

MUSIC PUBLISHERS

Edwin Ashdown Ltd 19 Hanover Square London W1

Augener (Galliard) 148 Charing Cross Road London WC2

Boosey and Hawkes Ltd 295 Regent Street London W1

Cambridge University Press (CUP) Bentley House 200 Euston Road London NW1

Chappell & Co Ltd 50 New Bond Street London W1

Doubleday & Co Inc (New York) 100 Wigmore Street London W1

Essex Music Ltd Dumbarton House 68 Oxford Street London W1

Galliard—see Augener

Longmans Green & Co Ltd 48 Grosvenor Street London W1

McDougall's Education Co (Holmes, McDougall) 30 Royal Terrace Edinburgh

Mills Music Ltd 20 Denmark Street London WC2

Novello & Co Ltd 27 Soho Square London W1

Oxford University Press (OUP) 44 Conduit Street London W1

Penguin Books Harmondsworth Middlesex

Robbins Music Corporation 35 Soho Square London W1

Schott & Co Ltd 48 Great Marlborough Street London W1

Theodore Presser Co Bryn Mawr Pennsylvania USA

Joseph Weinberger Ltd 33 Crawford Street London W1

36HH